D1289026

What's Inside a Rattlesnake's Rattle?

And Other Questions Kids Have About Snakes

by Heather L. Montgomery   illustrated by Bill Piggins

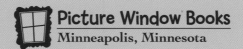

Picture Window Books
Minneapolis, Minnesota

Acknowledgments
This book was produced for Picture Window Books
by Bender Richardson White, U.K.

Illustrations by Bill Piggins
Consultant: John Stidworthy, Scientific Fellow of the Zoological Society,
London, and former Lecturer in the Education Department,
Natural History Museum, London

Picture Window Books
151 Good Counsel Drive
P.O. Box 669
Mankato, MN 56002-0669
877-845-8392
www.picturewindowbooks.com

Printed in the United States of America.

 All books published by Picture Window Books are manufactured
with paper containing at least 10 percent post-consumer waste.

Library of Congress Cataloging-in-Publication Data
Montgomery, Heather L.
What's inside a rattlesnake's rattle? : and other questions kids have
about snakes / by Heather L. Montgomery ; illustrated by Bill Piggins.
p. cm. — (Kids' questions)
Includes index.
ISBN 978-1-4048-5528-1 (library binding)
1. Rattlesnakes—Juvenile literature. 2. Snakes—Juvenile literature.
1. Piggins, Bill, ill. II. Title.
QL666.O69M66 2010
597.96—dc22   2009013011

SNAKES

Kids have lots of questions about snakes. What are they
made of? Do all snakes have fangs? What do they eat?
Can snakes swim? Do they have any enemies?
In this book, kids get answers.

What are snakes made of?

Dalton, age 7

Like your body, a snake's body is made of bones, muscles, a stomach, a heart, lungs, and a brain. But unlike you, a snake does not have hair. Instead, it has smooth, dry scales. A snake cannot keep its body warm. It must lie in sunlight to get warm.

How many kinds of snakes are there?

Ali, age 8

There are more than 2,900 kinds of snakes. Snakes live all around the world, except at the North and South Poles.

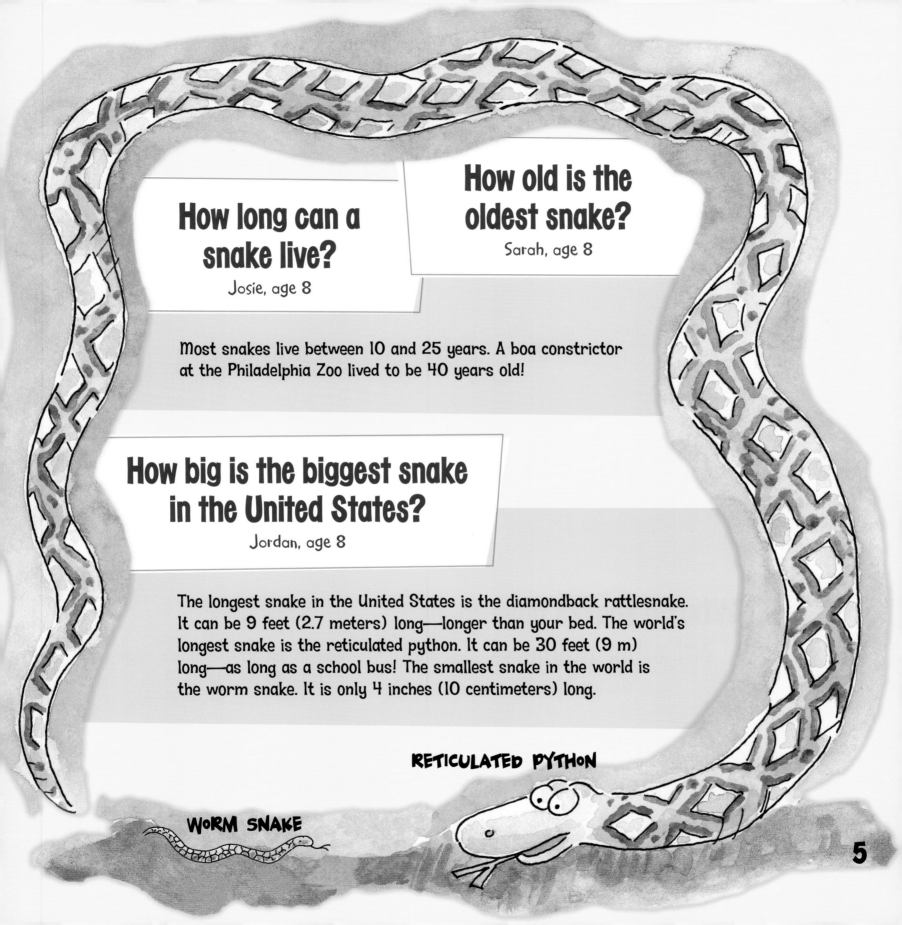

How long can a snake live?

Josie, age 8

How old is the oldest snake?

Sarah, age 8

Most snakes live between 10 and 25 years. A boa constrictor at the Philadelphia Zoo lived to be 40 years old!

How big is the biggest snake in the United States?

Jordan, age 8

The longest snake in the United States is the diamondback rattlesnake. It can be 9 feet (2.7 meters) long—longer than your bed. The world's longest snake is the reticulated python. It can be 30 feet (9 m) long—as long as a school bus! The smallest snake in the world is the worm snake. It is only 4 inches (10 centimeters) long.

RETICULATED PYTHON

WORM SNAKE

What do snakes eat?
Hannah, age 8

Do snakes eat human food?
Andy, age 8

Snakes are predators. They eat insects and animals such as mice, birds, fish, and other snakes. They also eat eggs. They do not eat food that people eat.

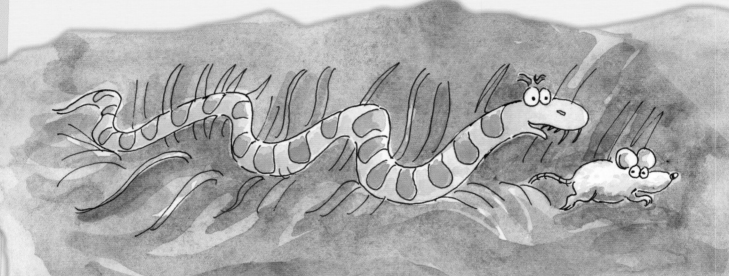

Why do snakes have to eat other animals?
Mia, age 8

Why do snakes eat mice?
Kevin, age 8

Snakes eat other animals, such as mice, to get energy. Mice eat grass seeds to get energy. The grass gets energy from the sun. This "food chain" keeps nature in balance. Each part of the chain depends on the other parts to live.

How big a thing can a snake eat?

Manuel, age 8

How do snakes eat big things?

Bereket, age 6

A large snake can eat a pig or even a crocodile! To do this, the bones in the snake's jaws and head come apart so its mouth can open wide. The teeth on the right side slide forward and sink into the food. Then the teeth on the left side slide forward.

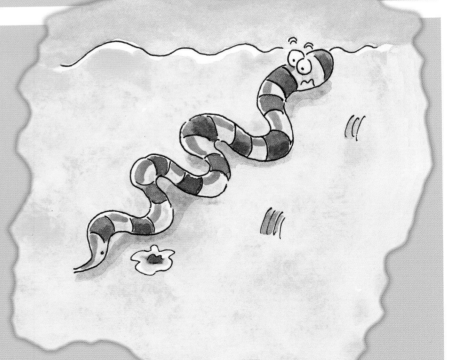

How do snakes go to the potty?

Jake, age 8

When snakes go potty, they use a hole near their tail. Their liquid and solid wastes come out of the same hole at the same time.

7

Do all snakes have fangs?

Seamus, age 7

No. Only certain types of snakes have fangs. Pythons and boa constrictors are snakes without fangs. Instead of poisoning their prey, they squeeze it.

Are all snakes poisonous?

Keara, age 7

How are snakes venomous?

Henry, age 8

No. Only certain types of snakes have venom. Venom is made in sacs above the jaws. When a snake bites, muscles squeeze the sacs. Venom then squirts through the snake's fangs and into the prey.

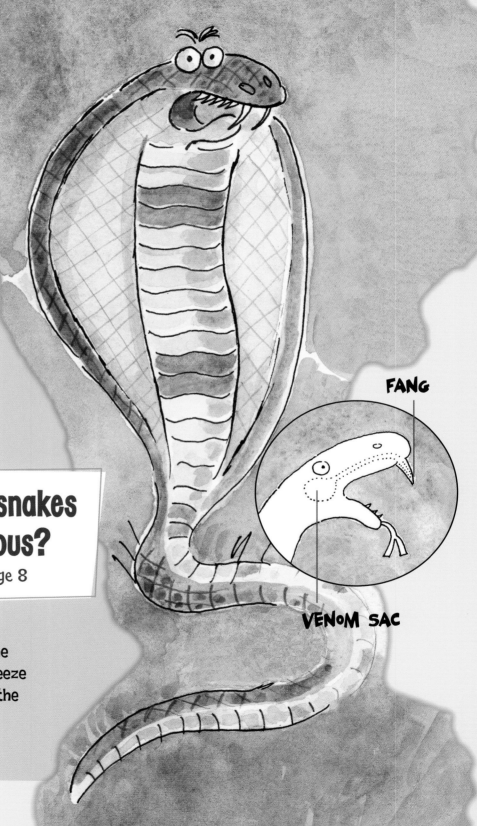

FANG

VENOM SAC

How do I know when they're venomous and not venomous?

Sabrina, age 8

It is hard to tell if a snake is venomous. In the United States, most poisonous snakes have a triangle-shaped head. Their eyes look like slits. But the venomous coral snake doesn't have either of these features.

Do snakes die when the poison gets in their mouth?

Jaina, age 8

No. Venom is only dangerous if it gets into the blood. Any venom a snake swallows is broken down by stomach acid, making it harmless.

Why don't snakes have legs?

Gabby, age 7

Snakes don't walk. They slide, creep, and swim to get around. Legs would get in the way as a snake wraps around a branch or goes underground.

SNAKE BACKBONE AND RIBS

How many bones does a snake have?

Hollister, age 7

A snake can have 1,000 bones. They help a snake bend and move around. Muscles connect to the bones. When the muscles shorten, the snake moves. The bones also protect a snake's organs, such as its heart, lungs, and brain.

Do snakes slither fast or slow?
Brianne, age 7

Are all snakes fast?
Seamus, age 7

Snakes are slower than they look. The coachwhip is one of the fastest snakes in North America. Even so, it can go only 5 miles (8 kilometers) per hour. You can run that fast!

Can snakes swim in deep water?
Abigale, age 8

Some can. Sea snakes have a flat tail that's perfect for swimming. Also, they can close their nostrils underwater. Sea snakes live in the warm waters of the Pacific and Indian Oceans.

How do snakes slither?

Loran, age 8

A snake uses the scales on the underside of its body to grab onto rocks, twigs, or dirt. It then pushes off that object and moves forward in a wavy motion.

How do snakes climb trees?

Kindergartners

To climb trees, snakes use the scales on the underside of their body to grip the bark. They stretch their head and body upward, grip the bark, and then pull their tail up, too.

Does a snake have ears?

Aaron, age 8

A snake does not have ears. But it does have ear bones! A snake uses its jaw to feel the ground shaking. The shaking wiggles the ear bones. Then the snake knows something is coming.

How do snakes find their prey in the dark?

Justin, age 8

Some snakes have special pits in their face. These pits can feel the heat of another animal's body. A rattlesnake, for example, can find a mouse in total darkness.

Can snakes smell with their nose?

Niko, age 8

Yes. A snake uses its nose to catch odors in the air. It also uses its tongue and mouth to smell things.

Do they always stick their tongues out?

Sara, age 6

Why do they have long tongues?

Hannah, age 7

A snake sticks out its tongue whenever it wants to smell. The long tongue catches odors in the air. The snake then touches its tongue to the roof of its mouth to smell the odor bits. When a snake smells food, it sticks out its tongue more often.

Why do snakes have sharp teeth?

Karsten, age 7

Snakes use their sharp teeth to hold on to their food, which may still be alive. Some snakes' teeth even curve backward. These teeth keep prey from crawling back out of the snake's mouth.

Why do they have a cut in their tongues?

Chris, age 8

A snake's split tongue helps it know where food is. The right tip stretches to the right. The left tip stretches left. If the left side of the tongue catches more odor bits, the snake knows the food is on the left side.

Why do snakes go *sssss*?

Kindergartners

Snakes make a hissing sound as a warning. The sound tells people and other animals to stay away.

15

Why do snakes desert their eggs?

Elaina, age 8

Some mother snakes lay their eggs and then leave them. The young snakes that hatch from those eggs can survive on their own. Other mother snakes guard their eggs. Still other snakes protect their eggs by keeping them inside their bodies. The eggs hatch inside, and the young snakes are born alive!

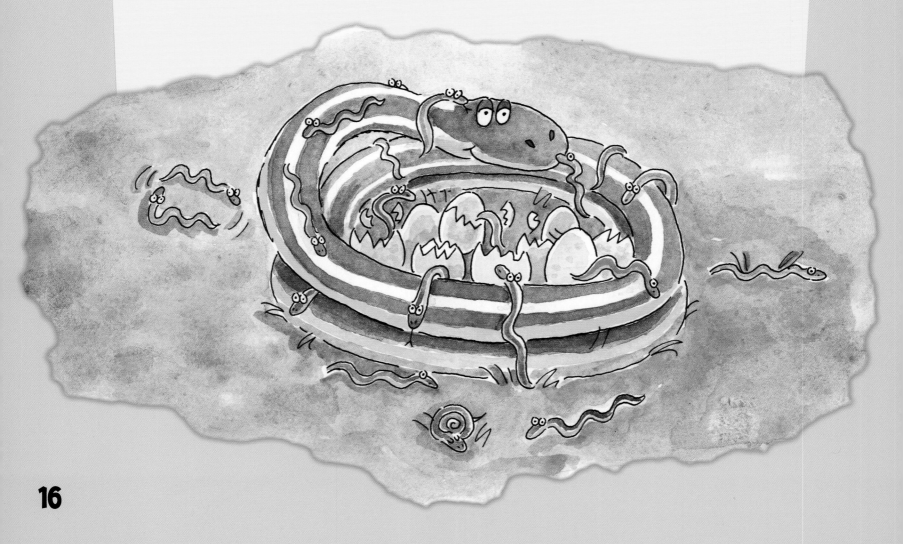

Do they bite when they're born?

Sarah, age 8

Yes. Young snakes act like their parents. They can bite and find food soon after they hatch.

Does a mother snake die when she has babies?

Madison, age 8

No. Usually snakes can lay eggs or give birth without any problems. In fact, the garter snake can lay as many as 70 eggs at a time and then do it again the next year!

How often do snakes shed their skin?

Corbin, age 8

A snake's skin protects it while it slides across rough rocks and bark. Whenever the snake gets too big for its skin, it sheds. The more a snake eats, the more often it will shed.

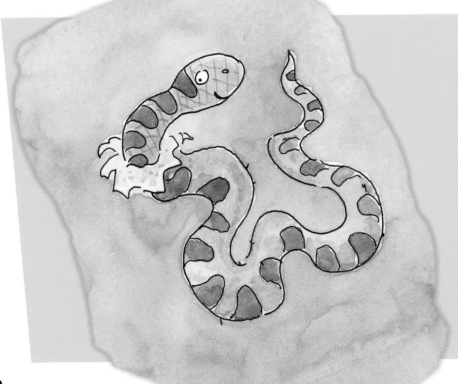

How do snakes shed their skin?

1st and 2nd graders

To shed its skin, a snake rubs its mouth or jaw against a stone until the skin splits. The snake then slides out of the skin, leaving it behind in one long piece. New skin has grown underneath.

What's inside a rattlesnake's rattle?

Aidan, age 7

There is nothing inside the rattle. The rattle is made of hollow rings of dry skin that hook together. The rings are made of keratin, the same stuff that makes up your fingernails. When the snake shakes its tail, the pieces of the rattle rub against each other. The rattling sound warns animals and people to stay away.

Can snakes squish me?
Giselle, age 8

Can poisonous snakes kill me?
Justin, age 6

Some can. A Burmese python could squish a person. The coral snake's venom can kill someone. But most snakes are harmless. Usually, snakes stay away from people. They eat smaller animals and avoid biting people. When a venomous snake has to bite to protect itself, it sometimes will not even use any venom.

Are some snakes vicious?
Andy, age 8

Are they all bad?
Dillon, age 7

Any snake may act vicious if it is in danger. It is not being bad. It is just protecting itself.

What snake should I stay away from the most?
Justin, age 8

Keep a safe distance away from any wild snake. In the United States, rattlesnakes are the most dangerous. In other parts of the world, stay away from spitting cobras. They can shoot venom almost 10 feet (3 m)!

What are snakes' enemies?

Justin, age 8

Snakes' natural enemies include hawks, opossums, skunks, and owls. But there are unnatural threats to snakes, too. Some people collect snakes for pets. Some people destroy snake habitats by building in them. Other people are scared of snakes and kill them.

Can I eat snakes?

Ethan, age 4

Yes. Some people in the United States eat rattlesnakes. Snake meat is especially popular in parts of Asia.

TO LEARN MORE

More Books to Read

Christiansen, Per. *Constrictor Snakes.* Pleasantville, N.Y.: Gareth Stevens Pub., 2009.

Simon, Seymour. *Giant Snakes.* San Francisco: Chronicle Books, 2006.

Somerville, Louisa. *Snakes.* Redding, Conn.: Brown Bear Books, 2009.

Thomson, Sarah L. *Amazing Snakes!* New York: HarperCollins Publishers, 2006.

Internet Sites

FactHound offers a safe, fun way to find Internet sites related to this book. All of the sites have been researched by our staff.

Here's all you do:

Visit *www.facthound.com*

FactHound will fetch the best sites for you!

GLOSSARY

fangs—curved, pointed upper teeth

habitat—the place where an animal naturally lives

jaw—a bone in the mouth to which teeth are connected

keratin—a material that is in a snake's skin and human hair and fingernails

predators—animals that hunt and eat other animals

prey—animals that are hunted and eaten by other animals

scales—small hard pieces of skin that cover a snake's body

venom—the poison that a snake shoots inside its prey

INDEX

Look for all of the titles in the Kids' Questions series:

Did Dinosaurs Eat People? And Other Questions Kids Have About Dinosaurs
What Is the Moon Made Of? And Other Questions Kids Have About Space
What's Inside a Rattlesnake's Rattle? And Other Questions Kids Have About Snakes
Why Do My Teeth Fall Out? And Other Questions Kids Have About the Human Body